First World War
and Army of Occupation
War Diary
France, Belgium and Germany

59 DIVISION
Divisional Troops
467 Field Company Royal Engineers
2 February 1917 - 16 July 1919

WO95/3017/2

The Naval & Military Press Ltd
www.nmarchive.com
Published in association with The National Archives

Published by

The Naval & Military Press Ltd

Unit 10 Ridgewood Industrial Park,

Uckfield, East Sussex,

TN22 5QE England

Tel: +44 (0) 1825 749494

www.naval-military-press.com

www.nmarchive.com

This diary has been reprinted in facsimile from the original. Any imperfections are inevitably reproduced and the quality may fall short of modern type and cartographic standards.

© **Crown Copyright**
Images reproduced by permission of The National Archives, London, England, 2015.

Contents

Document type	Place/Title	Date From	Date To
Heading	WO95/3017/2		
Heading	59th Division 467th Field Coy.R.E. Feb 1917-Dec 1918 July 1919		
War Diary	Durrington Camp.	02/02/1917	19/02/1917
War Diary	Southampton	20/02/1917	22/02/1917
War Diary	Le Havre	23/02/1917	28/02/1917
War Diary	Morcourt	01/03/1917	26/03/1917
War Diary	Estrees En. Chaussee	01/04/1917	09/04/1917
War Diary	Bernes.	10/04/1917	24/05/1917
War Diary	Equancourt	01/06/1917	04/06/1917
War Diary	Gouzeacourt Wood	01/06/1917	30/06/1917
War Diary	Metz	05/06/1917	08/07/1917
War Diary	Gouzeacourt Wood	01/07/1917	08/07/1917
War Diary	Equancourt	01/07/1917	09/07/1917
War Diary	Barastre Restcamp	08/07/1917	16/08/1917
War Diary	Le Transloy	16/08/1917	16/08/1917
War Diary	Forceville	23/08/1917	23/08/1917
War Diary	Barastre	31/07/1917	31/08/1917
War Diary	Ypres	09/09/1917	22/09/1917
War Diary	Vlamertinghe	22/09/1917	22/09/1917
War Diary	Ypres	23/09/1917	12/10/1917
War Diary	Crombeke	03/10/1917	03/10/1917
War Diary	Ablain	15/10/1917	31/10/1917
War Diary	Lievin	08/11/1917	11/11/1917
War Diary	Ablain	17/11/1917	23/11/1917
War Diary	Heudicourt	27/11/1917	27/11/1917
War Diary	Flesquires	29/11/1917	08/12/1917
War Diary	Trescault	08/12/1917	09/12/1917
War Diary	Flesquires	09/12/1917	09/12/1917
War Diary	Trescault	08/12/1917	13/12/1917
War Diary	Metz	15/12/1917	15/12/1917
War Diary	Trescault	20/12/1917	25/12/1917
War Diary	Dernier	28/12/1917	10/02/1918
Heading	467th Field Company March 1918		
War Diary	Noreuil	01/03/1918	01/03/1918
War Diary	Ervillers	01/03/1918	01/03/1918
War Diary	Noreuil	05/03/1918	12/03/1918
War Diary	Ervillers	19/03/1918	21/03/1918
War Diary	Ecoust	21/03/1918	29/03/1918
Heading	467th Field Company R.E April 1918		
War Diary		01/04/1918	31/05/1918
War Diary	Auchel	26/05/1918	10/06/1918
War Diary	Cauchy A La Tour	11/06/1918	30/06/1918
War Diary	Auchel	03/06/1918	03/06/1918
War Diary	Cauchy	19/06/1918	24/07/1918
War Diary	Grosville	27/07/1918	25/08/1918
War Diary	Bourecq	26/08/1918	27/08/1918
War Diary	Brayele	28/08/1918	03/09/1918
War Diary	Lestrum	04/09/1918	05/09/1918
War Diary	Pont Riquel	06/09/1918	04/10/1918

War Diary	Rouge De Bout	05/10/1918	20/10/1918
War Diary	Templeuve	21/10/1918	07/11/1918
War Diary	Sailly	08/11/1918	11/11/1918
War Diary	Mourcourt	12/11/1918	16/11/1918
War Diary	Thumesnil	17/11/1918	06/12/1918
War Diary	Barlin	07/12/1918	31/12/1918
War Diary	Hondeghem	01/01/1919	12/01/1919
War Diary	Dunkirk	13/01/1919	31/01/1919
War Diary	Mardyck Camp, Dunkirk	01/03/1919	16/07/1919

W0095 3017/2

59TH DIVISION

467TH FIELD COY. R.E.
FEB 1917-DEC 1918
JULY, 1919.

Army Form C. 2118.

WAR DIARY
or
INTELLIGENCE SUMMARY
(Erase heading not required.)

Vol I

Instructions regarding War Diaries and Intelligence Summaries are contained in F. S. Regs., Part II. and the Staff Manual respectively. Title Pages will be prepared in manuscript.

Place	Date	Hour	Summary of Events and Information	Remarks and references to Appendices
			February 1917 467th Field Coy R.E.	
DURRINGTON CAMP.	2nd		Company advance party (1 officer & 3 OR) left DURRINGTON CAMP for unknown	
"	4th		" " arrived in FRANCE.	
"	6th		A90166, Cpl Collyer H., admitted into No 25 General Hospital, HAVRE, with scabies.	
DURRINGTON CAMP.			During the first part of February the Company completed its equipment for overseas.	
DURRINGTON CAMP.	18th		10 Drivers, to complete establishment, arrived from Aldershot.	
DURRINGTON CAMP.	19th		Company left DURRINGTON CAMP for overseas, leaving 25 other ranks to bring details.	
SOUTHAMPTON.	20th & 21st		Company delayed at SOUTHAMPTON.	
SOUTHAMPTON	22nd		Company embarked at SOUTHAMPTON, on the "VIPER". A90057, Sapper Bennett, R. ≡ left behind at Rest Camp Hospital with chilled kidneys.	
LE HAVRE	23rd		Company disembarked, remained same day at LE HAVRE	
	24th		Company entrained at LONGEAU, and route marched to BLISY, spending night there.	
	25th		Company route marched from BLISY to HAMEL, spending night in hutment at HAMEL.	
	26th		A90059 Sapper Geiger E, left behind at BLISY, sick.	
	28th		Company marched from HAMEL to MORCOURT taking over billets at letter place from 118 Field Coy. Williams split into 3/1 Field Amb: Rest Station suffering from bronchitis.	

F. B. Jones
O/C 467th Field Coy, R.E. Major

2449 Wt. W14957/Mgo 750,000 1/16 J.B.C.I. & A. Forms/C.2118/12

WAR DIARY
INTELLIGENCE SUMMARY.
(Erase heading not required.)

Army Form C. 2118.

467 POMS Vol II

Hour, Date, Place	Summary of Events and Information	Remarks and references to Appendices
	March 1917. 467th Field Co. R.E.	
March 1.2.3. MORCOURT.	Whole Company in Billets.	
4th.	Advance party left for Hancourt to take over from outgoing Field Coy. This party spent night of 4th at FOUCAUCOURT. Inspection of Company by C.E. III Corps.	
5th.	Advance party arrived at N.20. c.3.8. Sheet 62 o.S.W.	
6th.	Company (Main body) left MORCOURT. Spent night at FOUCAUCOURT.	
7th.	Main body arrived at N.20. c.3.8. Sheet 62 c. S.W.	
15th.	490053. Sgt Innes W.W. killed in action by high explosive shell.	
16th.	do. buried at point. N.13. A.10.8. Map reference. DOMPIERRE. 62.C. S.W.I	
21st.	Company moved from N 20. c-3.8. 62 o.S.W. to ESTREE.	
24th.	490025. L/Cpl Watkins W.E. promoted to Acting Full Corporal. 490136. L.Cpl Lewis D.W. do " 2nd Corporal 490221. Sapper Snowden C. appointed " Lance Corporal.	
26th.	Company moved from ESTREE to MONS-EN-CHAUSSEE.	
	1st 2. Lieut. proceeded to FLEXECOURT for Infantry Course. D. B. Freer. Major O.C. 467th Field Co. R.E.	

Original
Army Form C. 2118.

WAR DIARY
or
INTELLIGENCE SUMMARY

461th Field Coy. R.E. April 1917.

(Erase heading not required.)

Place	Date April	Hour	Summary of Events and Information	Remarks and references to Appendices
ESTREES EN CHAUSSEE	1-9.		Company billeted in Dry Cuts.	
BERNES.	10:		Company moved from ESTREES to BERNES.	
BERNES.	17.		2nd Corpl W. N. 190196 reduced to rank of Sapper.	
	18.		Sr 190197. Sgt Lucas J.E. admitted to C.C. Station. do. do.	Struck off Strength
	24.		" 190151 Cpl Perkins S. do. do.	of Company from the
	24.		190121. S/pr Stacey. S.W. do. do.	dates shown.
			190099. S/pr Melton E.A. do. do.	
			190-106. S/pr Bullard J. do. do.	
			on 23.3.1917.	
	25		General work of Company:— Construction of road diversions round craters, repair of villas in BERNES; Erection of Queen and Adrian Huts; Mining and digging new posts on CORPS LINE; clearing roads in villages; co-operation with Infantry by two Sections R.E. which were attached to 119th Infantry Brigade.	

D. B. Freu
Major O.O.
467 Field Coy R.E.

ORIGINAL

Army Form C. 2118.

467 Field Coy
R.E. May 1917.

WAR DIARY
or
INTELLIGENCE SUMMARY.
(Erase heading not required.)

Instructions regarding War Diaries and Intelligence Summaries are contained in F.S. Regs., Part II. and the Staff Manual respectively. Title pages will be prepared in manuscript.

Hour, Date, Place		Summary of Events and Information	Remarks and references to Appendices
May 1-26.	BERNES.	Company in Huts, shelters, etc.	OC 4
May 22.	do.	2 Sections moved from BERNES to EQUANCOURT.	
May 26.	do	Remainder of Company do do.	
May 27.	do	2 Sections moved from EQUANCOURT to GOUZEAUCOURT WOOD.	
May 8.	BERNES.	Lt. R. Aly. Clutterbuck reported for duty.	
May 1.	do.	3 Reinforcements reported for duty from No. 8 Reinforcement C.R.E.	
May 6	do	3 do do No. 8 do do.	
May 17	do	2 do do No. 14 do do.	
May 24	do	2 do do No. 4 do do.	
		General work of Company.	
		General work of the Company has been erection of Adrian and Nissen Huts; construction of shelters; construction of rand deviavious round crater, and repair of roads.	

Basil C. Stacor
Capt: & Major OC
467 Field Co. R.E.

(73989) W4141—463. 400,000. 9/14. H.&J.Ltd. Forms/C. 2118/10.

Original

WAR DIARY

INTELLIGENCE SUMMARY. 461 Field Co. R.E. June 1917.

(Erase heading not required.)

Army Form C. 2118.

Hour, Date, Place	Summary of Events and Information	Remarks and references to Appendices
June 1-4. EQUANCOURT.	2 Sections and Mounted Section in huts, Shelters &c.	Vol 5
1-30. GOUZEACOURT WOOD	2 Sections hutted in huts, Shelters &c.	
5. METZ.	2 Sections and Coy. HQ moved from EQUANCOURT to METZ.	
17.	Section 2, relieved Section 3 in G. Wood.	
24.	Section 4 relieved Section 1 in G. Wood.	
1.	1 Reinforcement reported for duty from No.3 Res. Co. R.E.	
24.	do do No.4 do	
12.	No. 490141. C.Q.M.S. Chanter A. passed to No. 55. C.C.S. and struck off Strength of Company.	
24.	No. 490065. Sgt. Birch L. proceeded to England as a Candidate for Commission; Struck off Company Strength.	
23.	No. 490011. Lance Cpl. Chanplain S. slightly wounded by Shrapnel, and remained with Company.	
19.	No. 490026 Sapper Wood C. to 3rd C.C.S. Struck off Strength	
24.	No. 490222. Sapper Cuthbert J. to 48 C.C.S. do.	
15.	2nd Lieut Duffy J.S., slightly wounded by Shrapnel and passed to No. 55. C.C.S. Struck off Strength of Company June 16.	

(1)

Army Form C. 2118.

WAR DIARY (2)
=INTELLIGENCE SUMMARY=

(Erase heading not required.)

467 Field Co. R.E.
June 1917.

Hour, Date, Place	Summary of Events and Information	Remarks and references to Appendices
June 16 METZ.	2nd Lieut Blattwick A.g. Manced to N°55 C.S.S. on account of ill health. General Work of Company. Section of Divisional M.G. Carp at EQUANCOURT. Sections attached to Brigades in the line employed on digging advanced posts, and communication from front line to front line. Remainder of Company employed digging O.T., LINCOLN AVENUE, and laying trench boarding, etc.	

T. B. Jones
Major 10C
467 Field Co R.E.

ORIGINAL

Army Form C. 2118.

WAR DIARY
or
INTELLIGENCE SUMMARY

(Erase heading not required.)

467 Field Co R.E.

July 1917.

Vol 6

Place	Date	Hour	Summary of Events and Information	Remarks and references to Appendices
Gouzeaucourt & Metz	July 1-8		Company HQ and 2 Sections in huts shelling the METZ.	
Gouzeaucourt Wood	July 1-8		2 Sections in do do do	
Equancourt	July 1-9		Marched back in huts, shelling etc.	
	July 1-6		Section 1 moved from METZ to RoadCamp O.Q. BARASTRE.	
	" 8		Company HQ and Section 2,3 and 4 moved from METZ to Road Camp.	
	" 9		Moved section moved from EQUANCOURT to REST CAMP.	
BARASTRE REST CAMP	" 9		2/Lieut P.W. FYSH 2/Lieut M.H. JONES } Reported for duty and taken on strength of 2/Lieut P.H. LABDON. } Company from July 8. 1 Reinforcement reported for duty from No 8 Reinforcement 60Y. R.E.	
"	July 8.		490166. Sapper Boone W proceed to N° 21. 6 G.S. 490131. Sapper Smith A, sent to Base June 19. from N° 41 Stationery Hospital	All the new men shewn off the best having thought from the states shown.
"	" 9.			
"	July 18		490009. Sapper Boole f.B, proceed to N° 48. C.C.S. 490044. Sapper Murry B, proceed to N° 48. C.C.S.	
"	" 24		490047. L/Cple Preston A.B, proceed to N° 48 C.Q.S	
"	" 12		162620/ Private Rooks W.R. and 162996 Private Ennells W. of the 250th Divisional Employment Co attached for rations every 16 to hand at Waterpoint for duty	

General Work of the Company: Practically the whole Company has been employed in erecting permanent structures in Camp O.Q., such as huts, cookhouses, etc. A small amount of training has been carried out.

D. B. Frw.
Major OC
467 Field Co R.E.

ORIGINAL

WAR DIARY
or
INTELLIGENCE SUMMARY.

Army Form C. 2118.

467 Field Co. R.E. August 1917

(Erase heading not required.)

Instructions regarding War Diaries and Intelligence Summaries are contained in F.S. Regs., Part II. and the Staff Manual respectively. Title pages will be prepared in manuscript.

Hour, Date, Place		Summary of Events and Information	Remarks and references to Appendices
1917.			Vol 1
Aug 1-16.	BARASTRE	Company in REST CAMP billeted in tents, shelters, etc.	
" 16.	LE TRANSLOY	Company moved from BARASTRE to hutted camp LE TRANSLOY.	
" 23	FORCEVILLE.	Company moved from LE TRANSLOY to FORCEVILLE and billeted in houses, barns, etc.	
July 31	BARASTRE.	1. 490140. Sapper Bullivant. J. passed to 48.A.C.S. and struck off strength.	
Aug 4.	do	2. Sappers reported for duty from No. 4 Reinforcements and taken on strength of Company.	
Aug 7.	do	11. 2nd Lieut Gordon P.K. posted to 467 Field Co. R.E. and struck off strength of Company.	

General Work of Company.

The company has been employed in erection of huts, and general constructions of Winter Camps.

J.B. Shaw
Major
467 Field Co. R.E.

Army Form C. 2118.

Original

467 Field Co. R.E.
September 1914. Vol 8

WAR DIARY
or
INTELLIGENCE SUMMARY
(Erase heading not required.)

Instructions regarding War Diaries and Intelligence Summaries are contained in F. S. Regs., Part II. and the Staff Manual respectively. Title Pages will be prepared in manuscript.

Place	Date 1917	Hour	Summary of Events and Information	Remarks and references to Appendices
	Aug 31		Full Company entrained at AVELU and detrained at POPERINGHE Siding, marching by road to WINNEZEELE, and billeted in known site.	A.B.7.
YPRES.	Sept.8		Company marched from WINNEZEELE. Dismounted Section by lorries to YPRES, and billeted in dugout. Transport and Mounted Section moved by road to VLAMERTINGHE and billeted in empty horse lines.	A.B.7.
	Sept.10		Dismounted Section 1 moved from YPRES to VLAMERTINGHE.	A.B.7.
do	" 9		3. O.R. wounded by HE shell	A.B.7.
do	" 10		1. O.R. do do	A.B.7.
do	" 13		Dismounted Sections 2, 3 and 4 moved from dug outs to huts, shelter etc.	A.B.7.
do	" 19		Section 3 moved to VLAMERTINGHE and Section 1, Section 1 moved to YPRES.	A.B.7.
do	" 22		5. O.R. struck off Company strength	A.B.7.
VLAMERTINGHE	" 22		1. O.R. killed by HE shell	A.B.7.
do	" 22		4. O.R. wounded do.	A.B.6.7.
YPRES	" 23		Company HQ and Sections 1, 2 and 4 moved from huts and shelters to dug-outs.	A.B.7.
	" 25		Section 3 moved from VLAMERTINGHE to Dug-outs, YPRES, and this Company relieved the 432nd W. LANCS. F. Co. R.E., of the work in the WIELTJE sector. Map reference sheet 28. N.W. C.28.	A.B.7.

(1).

Original Army Form C. 2118.

(2) September continued

WAR DIARY
or
INTELLIGENCE SUMMARY
(Erase heading not required.)

Place	Date 1917	Hour	Summary of Events and Information	Remarks and references to Appendices
YPRES.	Sept 25		4. O.R. repords from R.E. Road Depot as Reinforcements and taken on the strength of the Company from that date.	A.13.7.
do	Sept 26		LIEVT. J.H.B. DIXON wounded by shell.	P.13.7.
do	Sept 26		7. O.R. wounded by splinters from H.E. shell, shrapnel.	A.13.7.
do	Sept 27		1. O.R. killed by H.E. shell	A.13.7.
do	do		7. O.R. wounded by do	A.B.13.7.
do	Sept 28		1. O.R. wounded by do	A.B.13.7.
do	do		5. O.R. gassed and burnt by Gas Shells. (Wounds)	A.B.13.7.
			Operations. The Company took part in the operations carried out by this Division (39th) on 26th instant, and were engaged in the repair of the WIELTJE - GRAVENSTAFEL road, EAST of the river STEENBEEK, and movements & evacuations on Zero day.	P.13.7.

WAR DIARY or INTELLIGENCE SUMMARY

Army Form C. 2118.

Original
467 Field Co. R.E.
September 1917 — Continued
No. 3

Place	Date	Hour	Summary of Events and Information	Remarks and references to Appendices
			Work of the month	
			The Company came under the command of 6. R.E. 11th Division on 4th instant, and was employed in the provision of Light and Shelter accommodation, and accessory buildings. On the night of the 42nd Division by the 9th Division, on 14th inst., the Company came under the command of the C.R.E. 9th Division and continued with the same work. On the 59th Division coming into the line at YPRES, the Company again came under the command of the C.R.E. 59th Division, and relieves the 422nd W. Laws 3. Co. R.E. in the WIELTJE sector on 23rd instant. From that date to the end of the month, the work of the Company was the repair of the WIELTJE - GRAVENSTAFEL road East of the road STEENBEEK. One Company of the 9th Hants Pioneers assisted the Company in this work from the 24th inst.	A.B.7.

B. Gill
467 F. Co. R.E.

B. Gill, Major O.C.

ORIGINAL DUPLICATE
467 Field Co. R.E.
October 1917

Vol 9

WAR DIARY
or
INTELLIGENCE SUMMARY
(Erase heading not required.)

Army Form C. 2118.

Instructions regarding War Diaries and Intelligence Summaries are contained in F. S. Regs., Part II. and the Staff Manual respectively. Title Pages will be prepared in manuscript.

Place	Date 1917	Hour	Summary of Events and Information	Remarks and references to Appendices
YPRES	Sept 28		14 O.R. sent to Hospital suffering from Gas burns.	B.C.D.
	29		1. O.R. died of wounds previous from Aeroplane Bomb-accidents.	B.C.D.
	29		1. O.R. wounded do.	B.C.D.
	30		2nd company moved from YPRES to VLAMERTINGHE.	B.C.D.
	Oct 1		do. VLAMERTINGHE to WATOU.	B.C.D.
	Oct 2		do. WATOU to SEATON CAMP. CROMBEKE.	B.C.D.
	Oct 4		do. CROMBEKE to STEENBECQUE.	B.C.D.
	Oct 7		do. STEENBECQUE to VERCHIN.	B.C.D.
	Oct 10		do. VERCHIN to PERNES.	B.C.D.
	Oct 11		do. PERNES to MAISNIL BOUCHÉ.	B.C.D.
	Oct 12		do. MAISNIL BOUCHÉ to ABLAIN St NAZAIRE, Company HQ and Mounted Section billetted in ABLAIN, in miscellaneous huts, shelters, etc. 1t Dismounted Section billetted in dugouts etc, LIEVIN.	B.C.D.
CROMBEKE	Oct 3.		2nd Lieut G.A. PICKERING reported for duty and taken on the strength of the Co. from 6th	B.C.D.
—	Oct 3.		1. O.R. still from wounds (Gas) at N° 16 C.C.S.	B.C.D.
ABLAIN	Oct 15		4. O.R. reported from R.E. Base Depot as reinforcements and taken on the strength of the Company from Oct 15.	B.C.D.
Do	Oct 18.		N° A90103. Sergt DOWNES. G.A. proceeded to England for Commission in R.E.	B.C.D.
Do.	Oct 19		24. O.R. reported from R.E. Base Depot as reinforcements and taken on the strength of the Company from Oct 19	B.C.D.
Do	Oct 22		10. O.R. ditto from Oct 22.	B.C.D.

(1)

Army Form C. 2118.

WAR DIARY
or
INTELLIGENCE SUMMARY
(Erase heading not required.)

467 Field Co. R.E.

October 1917.

Place	Date	Hour	Summary of Events and Information	Remarks and references to Appendices
Ypres			General work of the month. The Company moved out of the YPRES area on Sept 30 1917 into various rest camps and billets as shown, thence into forward area of LENS. The whole of the Dranoutre Hutons (with the exception shewn below) have been employed from Oct 13th onwards, in clearing out, and laying duckboards in, ABSALOM O.T, machine gun shelt 36.0.S.W. M24. d.4.9. and in CROCODILE C.T. at M.24.a.3.5. (Excepting a party of 5 O.R. worked at N.19.c.9.1 on clearing out and connecting up cellars. A party of 16 O.R. have been employed at Coy. HQ ABLAIN, in clearing, repairing and painting all Transport, which was badly in need of repairs, ready for the winter months. Also in cleaning and repairing roads to enhance of camp, and making suitable standings for horses at water front.	

Ypres 28 X 17

Niel C. Deacon
Captain for OC
467 Field Co. R.E.

Original

Army Form C. 2118.

WAR DIARY
or
~~INTELLIGENCE SUMMARY.~~ 467. Field Coy. RE NOVEMBER 1917

(Erase heading not required.)

Instructions regarding War Diaries and Intelligence Summaries are contained in F.S. Regs., Part II. and the Staff Manual respectively. Title pages will be prepared in manuscript.

Hour, Date, Place		Summary of Events and Information	Remarks and references to Appendices
ABLAIN.	July 27/17.	49227 a/s/and Syt Jones S.R. struck off strength, on being transferred to H.Q. 3rd Army.	P.B.9.
Do.	Oct 28.	1. O.R. evacuated sick and struck off strength.	P.B.9.
	Oct 31.	Number 490.055 Sergt JACOB BROOKS and Number 490061 Corporal WILLIAM STAINSBY awarded the Military Medal, authority 59 Div. R.O. 727. 31.10.17.	P.B.9.
LIEVIN	Nov 3/9.	1. O.R. wounded in back by shrapnel.	P.B.9.
	Nov 8.	Company H.Q. moved from ABLAIN to LIEVIN	P.B.9.
LIEVIN	Nov 8.	1. O.R. Reinforcement arrived and taken on strength.	P.B.9.
	" 9	3 O.R. do	P.B.9.
	" 10	2 O.R. do	P.B.9.
	" 11.	1. O.R. Evacuated sick and struck off strength.	P.B.9.
ABLAIN.	" 17.	Company H.Q. and 4 Dismounted Sections moved from LIEVIN to ABLAIN, handing over to 1st Canadian Divnl Engineers.	P.B.9.
	19	do	P.B.9.
	21.	Full Company moved from ABLAIN to GOUY-EN-ARTOIS.	P.B.9.
	23	GOUY to COURCELLES.LE.COMTE.	P.B.9.
	25.	COURCELLES to HEUDECOURT.	P.B.9.
		2. O.R. Reinforcements arrived and taken on strength.	P.B.9.

①

Original.

Army Form C. 2118.

WAR DIARY
or
INTELLIGENCE SUMMARY.
(Erase heading not required.)

Instructions regarding War Diaries and Intelligence Summaries are contained in F.S. Regs., Part II. and the Staff Manual respectively. Title pages will be prepared in manuscript.

Hour, Date, Place	Summary of Events and Information	Remarks and references to Appendices
#	(2)	
HEUDICOURT. Nov 29.	The Company moved from HEUDICOURT to FLESQUIERS and billeted in ellais de.	→ B.9.
	2 horses killed by shell fire.	
FLESQUIERS Nov 29.	2. O.R. Reinforcements arrived and taken on strength.	→ B.9.
	General work of the Company	
	The main work of the Company has been the clearing of the 2 main C.Ts. in the LENS Sector, namely; CROCODILE and ABSALOM, providing drainage, and laying duckboards in same. Construction of dump hands in SUPPORT LINE and the mapping and reinforcing of cellars for N.Ks. Accommodation.	→ B.9.

→ B. Irving
Major OC
A67 J.Co. RE

WAR DIARY or INTELLIGENCE SUMMARY.

Army Form C. 2118.

467 Field Coy R.E.   December 1917

Place	Date	Hour	Summary of Events and Information	Remarks and references to Appendices
FLESQUIRES	Dec 1st		Full Company billetted in barns cellars etc	B.C.D.
Do	Dec 1st		2.O.R. Reinforcements reported from Base and taken on strength	B.C.D.
Do	Dec 2		1 Horse killed by shell fire	B.C.D.
Do	Dec 4		2.O.R. Reinforcements from Base and taken on strength	B.C.D.
Do	Dec 5		Mounted kitchen and Transport moved from FLESQUIRES to TRESCAULT	B.C.D.
Do	Dec 6		1.O.R. wounded by shell fire	B.C.D.
Do	Dec 7		1.O.R. do	B.C.D.
Do	Dec 9		3.O.R. wounded by "Shell gas"	B.C.D.
TRESCAULT	Dec 8		1 Horse killed by shell fire	B.C.D.
Do	Dec 8		Mounted Section and Transport moved from TRESCAULT to METZ	B.C.D.
Do	Dec 9		H.Q. and 4 Sections moved from FLESQUIRES to TRESCAULT	B.C.D.
FLESQUIRES	Dec 9		1.O.R. wounded by shell fire	B.C.D.
TRESCAULT	Dec 12		3.O.R. Reinforcements from Base and taken on strength of Coy	B.C.D.
Do	Dec 13		3.O.R. do	B.C.D.
METZ	Dec 15		1. L.D. Horse died from wounds	B.C.D.
TRESCAULT	Dec 20		1.O.R. died of wounds received from shell fire	B.C.D.
Do	Dec 21		1.O.R. wounded by shell fire	B.C.D.

Army Form C. 2118.

WAR DIARY
or
INTELLIGENCE SUMMARY.
(Erase heading not required.)

Instructions regarding War Diaries and Intelligence Summaries are contained in F. S. Regs., Part II. and the Staff Manual respectively. Title pages will be prepared in manuscript.

Original

Place	Date	Hour	Summary of Events and Information	Remarks and references to Appendices
	Dec 22		2.	
			HQ and 4 Sections moved from TRESCAULT to BARASTRE	B.C.D.
	Do		Mounted Section own movement do NETZ to Do.	B.C.D.
	Dec 24		do do BARASTRE to ACHIET LE PETIT.	B.C.D.
	Dec 25		do do ACHIET to DERNIER.	B.C.D.
	Dec 25		HQ and 4 Sections do BARASTRE to DERNIER.	B.C.D.
DERNIER	Dec 28		I.O.R. reinforcement reported for duty from Base ossistaken on length.	B.C.D.
			General North of the Company	
			The main work of the Company has been the construction of the first line of defence round the village of FLESQUIRES, and the conversion of a captured German trench into third line of defence North of the village of	
			TRESCAULT. Company moved into real billets at DERNIER on	B.C.D.
	Dec 25/17			B.C.D.
			Basil C Steven	
			Capt for Major O.C	
			467 Field Co. R.E.	

A.5834. Wt. W4973/M687. 750,000. 8/16. D. D. & L. Ltd. Forms/C.2118/13.

WAR DIARY
INTELLIGENCE SUMMARY

467 Field Co. R.E. Army Form C. 2118.

January 1918. ORIGINAL

(Erase heading not required.)

Instructions regarding War Diaries and Intelligence Summaries are contained in F.S. Regs., Part II. and the Staff Manual respectively. Title pages will be prepared in manuscript.

Hour, Date, Place	Summary of Events and Information	Remarks and references to Appendices
DENIER. Jan 1-28 inclusive	The Company has been billetted in various barns, rooms, etc., in DENIER, as a rest station as shewn	
Jan 1st.	4 O.R. reported as reinforcements and taken on the strength of the Company	B.C.D.
" 11th	4 do	B.C.D.
" 13th	3 do	B.C.D.
" 22nd	5 do	B.C.D.
" 25	5 do	B.C.D.
	General Work of the month	
	Practically the whole of the Company has been employed in carrying out repairs to billets in neighbouring villages, etc. A small amount of training has been carried out whenever possible.	B.C.D.

Reid. C. Bacon Captain acting O.C.

Original

WAR DIARY
or
INTELLIGENCE SUMMARY
(Erase heading not required.)

467. Field C.oy R.E.

February 1918.

Army Form C. 2118

Instructions regarding War Diaries and Intelligence Summaries are contained in F. S. Regs., Part II. and the Staff Manual respectively. Title Pages will be prepared in manuscript.

Place	Date 1918	Hour	Summary of Events and Information	Remarks and references to Appendices
	Jany 29		The Company moved from its billets at DENIER to BERLES.	A.B.F.
	" 30		Company HQ and Dismounted sections moved from BERLES to ERVILLERS.	A.B.F.
	Feb 3		Transport and Mounted section moved from BERLES to BAILLEUVAL.	A.B.F.
	Feb 6		1 O.R. reported from Base as Reinforcement and taken on the strength of the Company.	A.B.F.
	" 5		No. 490037 Lance Corpl GRAHAM J.W. awarded the "BELGIAN CROIX DE GUERRE" as per 59th Divue Routine Order 961 5/2/1918.	A.B.F.
	" 10		Company HQ & 3 sections moved from ERVILLERS to NOREUIL and billetted in Caves, dugouts, etc.	A.B.F.

General Works of the Company: From 1st Feb to the 10th the Company were employed in repair work in Show Area, and this is still being carried on by 1 Section R.E. Work in line consists of making dug outs, digging new trenches, constructing an Advanced Dressing Station, Baby Elephant Shelters, wiring, etc.

A. B. Ferns.
Major O.C.
467 F.Coy R.E.

59th Division.

WAR DIARY

467th FIELD COMPANY R. E.

MARCH 1 9 1 8

1. 59 Originals
Sheet 1.
467th Field Coy R.E.
MARCH, 1918.
Vol 14

WAR DIARY
or
INTELLIGENCE SUMMARY
(Erase heading not required.)

Army Form C. 2118

Instructions regarding War Diaries and Intelligence Summaries are contained in F.S. Regs., Part II. and the Staff Manual respectively. Title Pages will be prepared in manuscript.

Place	Date	Hour	Summary of Events and Information	Remarks and references to Appendices
NOREUIL	MARCH		Coy. H.Q. & 3 sections at NOREUIL; 1 section and transport lines at ERVILLERS.	To. B. Q. 9.
ERVILLERS	MAR. 1		Lieut M.H. JONES to hospital, sick.	A. B. 9.
NOREUIL	MAR. 5		1 O.R. wounded by shell fire.	A. B. 9.
	MAR. 11		Coy. H.Q. & 3 section moved from NOREUIL to ERVILLERS, billeted in hutted camp.	A. B. 9.
NOREUIL	MAR. 12		1 O.R. wounded by shell fire.	A. B. 9.
ERVILLERS	MAR. 19		1 O.R. (Sapper) reinforcement, reported.	A. B. 9.
	MAR. 20		3 section moved to ECOUST, billeted in shelters dug out.	A. B. 9.
ERVILLERS	MAR. 21		7 O.R. (6 sappers, 1 driver) reinforcements, reported.	A. B. 9.
ECOUST	MAR. 21		1 C.S.M. killed by shell fire	A. B. 9.
			2 O.R. missing } German attack commenced, 2pm.	A. B. 9.
			1 O.R. wounded remains	
			2 O.R. gassed.	
			3 O.R. wounded – present	
			Mounted section moved from ERVILLERS to AYETTE, thinned here	
	MAR. 21		3 sections to ERVILLERS (from line behind ECOUST) and on to AYETTE, meanwhile bivouacs	A. B. 9.
	MAR. 22		Coy. moved to AVELUY, to Hutted Camp.	A. B. 9.
	MAR. 23		Coy. moved to PONT NOYELLES, billeted in barn.	A. B. 9.
	MAR. 25		Coy. moved to MONTRELET, billeted in barn.	A. B. 9.
	MAR. 26		Coy. addressed by G.O.C. while at MONTRELET.	A. B. 9.
			Dismounted section moved by rail to CAUCOURT, billeted in huts	
	MAR. 28			
	MAR. 29		Mounted section moved to MAISNIL (ST POL), billeted in barn.	To. B. 9.
	MAR. 29		" " CAUCOURT, billeted in hut.	To. B. 9.

Army Form C. 2118

WAR DIARY
or
INTELLIGENCE SUMMARY

(Erase heading not required.)

Sheet 2.

Instructions regarding War Diaries and Intelligence Summaries are contained in F.S. Regs., Part II. and the Staff Manual respectively. Title Pages will be prepared in manuscript.

Place	Date	Hour	Summary of Events and Information	Remarks and references to Appendices
	1918. MARCH		General work of the month. Work was of a general nature much as dug outs, Dressing station, accommodation for gunners of trenches, construction of Battle Zone trenches, etc.	A.B.?

D. B. Long.
Major,
O.C.

59th Divisional Engineers

467th FIELD COMPANY R. E.

APRIL 1918.

Original

Army Form C. 2118.

467 Field Coy. R.E.

April, 1918.

WAR DIARY
INTELLIGENCE SUMMARY
(Erase heading not required.)

Instructions regarding War Diaries and Intelligence Summaries are contained in F. S. Regs., Part II. and the Staff Manual respectively. Title Pages will be prepared in manuscript.

Place	Date	Hour	Summary of Events and Information	Remarks and references to Appendices
	Mar 31		Mounted Section march from CAUCOURT to ECQUEDECQUES.	B.C.D.
	Apr 1		Dismounted Section move from CAUCOURT to TRAPPISTE CAMP, entraining at HOUDAIN and detraining at PROVEN	B.C.D.
	" 2		Mounted Section travel from ECQUEDECQUES to MORBECQUE	B.C.D.
	" 3		Mounted Section arrived at TRAPPISTE CAMP, WATOU.	B.C.D.
			1 Officer and 9 O.R. reported from R.E. Base Depot.	B.C.D.
	" 4		Dismounted section move to YPRES by light railway from POPERINGHE.	B.C.D.
	" 4		Mounted " " " "	B.C.D.
	" 7		1 OR reinforcement from R.E. Base Depot.	B.C.D.
	" 8		" " " "	B.C.D.
	" 12		Coy. march from YPRES to VLAMERTINGHE.	B.C.D.
	" 12		Dismounted Section move to ROIEWAERSVELDE by rail from BRANDHOEK.	B.E.D.
	" 13		" " " " LOCRE.	B.C.D.
	" 14		" " " LOCRE from VLAMERTINGHE.	B.C.D.
	" 14		Mounted " " " BAILLEUL + All reserve line there, losing 5 O.R. wounded	B.C.D.
	" 15		Dismounted " " " WESTOUTRE.	B.C.D.
	" 15		" " " ABÉÉLE from LOCRE.	B.C.D.
	" 16		Mounted section march to RENINGHELST.	B.C.D.
	" 16		Coy: march from WESTOUTRE and RENINGHELST to billets near TERDEGHEM.	B.C.D.
	" 18		" " TERDEGHEM to INTERNATIONAL CORNER.	B.C.D.
	" 19		" " INTERNATIONAL CORNER to FARMS in HOUTKERQUE area.	B.C.D.
	" 21		" " to Camp near ST JANSTER BIEZEN.	B.C.D.
	" 27		" " " to BUSSEBOOM DUMP near RENINGHELST - POPERINGHE ROAD.	B.C.D.
	" 29		Dismounted section travel to " " "	B.C.D.

Army Form C. 2118.

WAR DIARY
~~INTELLIGENCE SUMMARY~~ Sheet 2.
(Erase heading not required.)

Instructions regarding War Diaries and Intelligence Summaries are contained in F. S. Regs., Part II. and the Staff Manual respectively. Title Pages will be prepared in manuscript.

Place	Date	Hour	Summary of Events and Information	Remarks and references to Appendices
General work.			The Company have been engaged during the month on improvement of tracks, making strong points, spare parts for demolition of bridges at YPRES, digging Corps line of HERZEELE and RESERVE LINE in front of POPERINGHE. B.C.D.	

Basil C. Mason, Capt.
for O.C.
467 (N.M.) FIELD COMPANY, R.E.

ORIGINAL

Army Form C. 2118.

Vol 16

WAR DIARY
of
467. Field Coy. R.E. (T.F.)
INTELLIGENCE SUMMARY.
MAY. 1918.

(Erase heading not required.)

Instructions regarding War Diaries and Intelligence Summaries are contained in F.S. Regs., Part II and the Staff Manual respectively. Title pages will be prepared in manuscript.

Hour, Date, Place	Summary of Events and Information	Remarks and references to Appendices
1918. May 1 – 6.	Coy (Dismounted) billeted in huts at BUSSE-BOOM.	A.B.7.
"	" (Mounted) Tents at ST JEAN DE BIEZEN.	A.B.7.
6th.	Dismounted Sections moved from BUSSE-BOOM to HOUTKERQUE. Mounted Section " ST.J. DE. BIEZEN to "	A.B.7. A.B.7.
7th.	Dismounted Sections moved by bus from HOUTKERQUE to ST OMER.	A.B.7.
8th.	" " by road from HOUTKERQUE to ROBECQ.	A.B.7.
	Transport moved by road from ROBECQ to ST. OMER.	A.B.7.
9th.	Full Company moved by road from ST OMER to REBECQ.	A.B.7.
10th.	" " " " REBECQ to FIEFS.	A.B.7.
11th.	" " " " FIEFS to AVOHEL.	A.B.7.
11th to 31st.	" " billeted in huts at AVOHEL.	A.B.7.
26th AVOHEL.	1.O.R. reported as reinforcement from R.E. Base Depot on Co.S.M. and taken on strength of Coy from that date.	A.B.7.
	GENERAL WORK. The Company has chiefly been employed in the construction of B. sector on the B.B. line. Other work has been carried out such as, Erection of huts, Cookhouses etc. T.B. Farr. Major O.C.	A.B.7.

467 (N.M.)
FIELD COMPANY,
R.E.
No.
Date May 31st 1918

(73989) W4141—463. 400,000. 9/14. H.&J.Ltd. Forms/C. 2118/10.

ORIGINAL

WAR DIARY
or
INTELLIGENCE SUMMARY.
(Erase heading not required.)

467 Field Coy R.E. T.F. Army Form C. 2118.

JUNE 1918.

Hour, Date, Place	Summary of Events and Information	Remarks and references to Appendices
JUNE 1918.		
1st 10th AUCHEL.	Company situated in huts.	A.B.7.
11h. No. 3 Oh. CAUCHY. A la TOUR.	Sect of Company moved from AUCHEL to tented camp in CAUCHY A la TOUR.	A.B.7.
3rd AUCHEL.	Extract from Supplement to "London Gazette" dated June 3rd. HONOURS and REWARDS. The Military Cross. Lt. Major C.B. Lew.	A.B.7.
	5.7. D.A.O. 1289 dated 24.6.1918.	A.B.7.
19th CAUCHY.	1 O.R. reinforcement arrived from R.E. Base Depot and taken on acting W. of Company accordingly	A.B.7.
30th CAUCHY.	1 O.R. do	A.B.7.
	General Work. The Company has been employed in the construction of the "B" sector of the 18 B. line, and the supervision of three German Prisoners Battalions employed on this Work; towards the end of the month these were replaced by one Chinese Labour Company.	A.B.7.

A.B. Lew
Major R.E.

467 (N.M.)
FIELD COMPANY.
R.E.
No.
Date.

ORIGINAL.

Army Form C. 2118.

WAR DIARY of 467 Field Co. R.E. 1F.
INTELLIGENCE SUMMARY. July 1918.

(Erase heading not required.)

Instructions regarding War Diaries and Intelligence Summaries are contained in F.S. Regs., Part II and the Staff Manual respectively. Title pages will be prepared in manuscript.

Hour, Date, Place		Summary of Events and Information	Remarks and references to Appendices
1918 July 1.	22 mm.	Full Company in tented camp at CAUCHY: A LA TOUR.	↑ B.9.
" 5.	CAUCHY.	1 O.R. Reinforcement reported from Base and taken on strength.	↑ B.1.
" 12.	Do.	14 O.R. do.	↑ B.1.
" 23.		Dismounted sections moved by motor lorries from CAUCHY. A. LA. TOUR to WARLUZEL. Mounted section and transport moved by road to CHELERS.	↑ B.1.
" 24.		Dismounted sections moved by route march from WARLUZEL to GROSVILLE. Mounted section and transport moved by road from CHELERS to GROSVILLE.	↑ B.1.
" 27.	GROSVILLE.	21 O.R. Reinforcements reported from Base and taken on strength.	↑ B.2.
		General Work. July. 22 midnight. The Company has been employed in the construction of the B. sector of the B.B. Line, and the supervising of one Chinese Labour Company employed in this sector. July 25-31. The Company has been occupied with the repair of trenches etc in the forward areas.	↑ B.2. ↑ B.2.

↑ B. Pan.
Major. O.C.

467 (M.)
FIELD Co. PANY.

No. ....
Date ....

WAR DIARY 467 FIELD Cᵒʸ R.E.(T.F.)

Sheet 1

INTELLIGENCE SUMMARY. — August 1918.

Army Form C. 2118. ORIGINAL

Place	Date	Hour	Summary of Events and Information	Remarks and references to Appendices
GROSVILLE.	1st		2/ LIEUT. G.A. PICKERING. Posted to 467 FIELD Cᵒʸ R.E. (T.F.) The main work was the running and clearing of Mann O.P. in forward area. Weather normal. Enemy shelling Nil	A.B.9.
Do.	2nd		do.	A.B.9.
Do.	3rd		Laying of duckboards in Main O.P. and section of track in main line of advance. Very wet weather. No enemy action.	A.B.9.
Do.	4th		do.	A.B.9.
Do.	5th		Sappers shifts employed running Mann O.P., laying duckboards in same, erecting footelips in FIFE AV. Weather very wet. Enemy shelling NIL.	A.B.9.
Do.	6th		do. Weather NORMAL. No enemy action	A.B.9.
Do.	7th		do. running Mann O.P., erecting footelips in outpost line. Weather normal.	A.B.9.
Do.	8th		do., also salving R.E. stores.	A.B.9.
Do.	9th		do.	A.B.9.
Do.	10th		Chief work is running sides of O.P. and laying duckboards in same, salving R.E. stores.	A.B.9.
Do.	11th		do.	A.B.9.
Do.	12th		do.	A.B.9.

Army Form C. 2118.

WAR DIARY
or
INTELLIGENCE SUMMARY.
(Erase heading not required.)

Sheet 2.

Instructions regarding War Diaries and Intelligence Summaries are contained in F. S. Regs., Part II. and the Staff Manual respectively. Title pages will be prepared in manuscript.

Place	Date Aug	Hour	Summary of Events and Information	Remarks and references to Appendices
GROSVILLE	13th		1.0.R. Reinforcement reported from R.E. Base Depot and taken on strength of Coy. Company is chiefly at work on cutting and erecting jump-ups in hut operations. Running, levelling, ramming main C.T.s and laying duckboards in Saulty. Salvaging R.E. Stores. Patrolling LIGHT. RAILWAY. WEATHER. Normal. ENEMY ACTION Nil.	A.B.T.
Do.	14th		Do. Do.	A.B.T.
Do.	15th		Do. Do. Do. Slight shelling – no Casualties	A.B.T.
Do.	16th		Russian Sap Commenced. Running near C.T.s. Excavating new Coy HQrs. Do. observing action	A.B.T.
Do.	17th		" " continued do. Do Do	A.B.T.
Do.	18th		1.0.R. Reinforcement reported from R.E. Base Depot and taken on strength of Coy. Work, chiefly levelling main C.T.s, salvaging R.E. Stores Etc. Patrolling light Railway. Do.	A.B.T.
Do	19th		" " show Coy H.Q.s cleaning hum. " " Do	A.B.T.
Do	20th		do. " Issuing urinal boards, fixing gas curtains, laying duckboards " Do	A.B.T.
Do	21st		" Excavating sap to M.G.E., show Coy HQs. Do Salving R.E. materials Do	A.B.T.
Do	22nd		Coy erected 12 Infantry Bridges over a section of the front line, and laid out a jumping off tape for the attack by the 52nd DIVISION on morning of Aug 23rd. Weather normal. Enemy shelling slight no Casualties	A.B.T.
Do	23d.		Devonvale Echelons moved by route march from GROSVILLE to SAULTY and were billeted in bivouacs. Weather showery towards night.	A.B.T.

WAR DIARY
or
INTELLIGENCE SUMMARY.

Army Form C. 2118.

Sheet 3

(Erase heading not required.)

Place	Date Aug	Hour	Summary of Events and Information	Remarks and references to Appendices
	23rd		Transport and dismounted section moved by road from GROSVILLE to NUNCQ and were billeted in barns &c.	A.B.7.
	24th		" " NUNCQ to MONCHY. (ST POL).	A.B.7.
	25th		Dismounted Sections moved by train from SAULTY to AIRE, arriving there at 11.50 hours. Thence taken by motor lorries to BOURECQ. NORMAL weather.	A.B.7.
			Transport and dismounted section moved by road from MONCHY to BOURECQ. NORMAL weather.	A.B.7.
BOURECQ	26.		Company billeted in barns, shelters &c.	A.B.7.
	27.		Still company paraded, and prepared for move forward 29th. Weather showery.	A.B.7.
			" moved by road from BOURECQ to BRAYELLE, near ST VENANT, and are billeted in Cottages etc. Weather normal.	A.B.7.
BRAYELLE	28		Sappers employed on repairs to huts, repairs to billets, erection of Nissen Huts and preparing accommodation for reinforcements.	A.B.7.
Do	29		Do	A.B.7.
Do	30		Do	A.B.9.

NOTE:— The Company has had no casualties during this month.

J.B.Frew
Major OC.
467 FIELD CO. R.E. T.F.

ORIGINAL
Army Form C. 2118.

WAR DIARY 1 — 467 FIELD. COY. R.E.
INTELLIGENCE SUMMARY September 1918.
(Erase heading not required.)

Vol 20

Place	Date 1918	Hour	Summary of Events and Information	Remarks and references to Appendices
	Aug 31		Company in billets at BRAYELLE, and commenced construction of bridge for foot bridge traffic over LA LAWE river, and footbridge over forward roads on arrival at BEAUPRE. Other sections repairing and fixing up shell hole etc, on forward roads, with two Companies of Pioneers which were permanently attached to this Company for work on roads. There was heavy enemy shell fire whilst the men were working which largely hindered progress, also rain at night. No casualties.	A.B.T.
BRAYELLE	Sept 1st.		Bridge completed about 8 a.m. after working through night of Aug 31-Sept 1. Repair of forward roads continued. Weather dry. Enemy shell fire still active. No casualties.	A.B.T.
Do.	2nd		8 ton bridge over LA LAWE river commenced. Forward posts towards LA GORGUE repaired. Weather fine. Enemy quiet.	A.B.T.
Do.	3rd.		Divisional Sections and Coy. HQrs moved by road to LESTREM and bivouaced. Construction of 8 ton bridge continued. Repairs of roads from LA GORGUE to ESTAIRES, and washing fields for Coy. Weather hot. Enemy quiet.	A.B.T.
LESTREM	4th	Nil	8 ton bridge completed. Repairs to Camp for 59 Divnl School and erection of hut etc. for Divnl Water Factory at LUCHEUX. Weather hot. Enemy action. NIL.	A.B.T.

Army Form C. 2118.

WAR DIARY
Sheet 2
INTELLIGENCE SUMMARY
September 1918

(Erase heading not required.)

Instructions regarding War Diaries and Intelligence Summaries are contained in F. S. Regs., Part II. and the Staff Manual respectively. Title Pages will be prepared in manuscript.

Place	Date 10/18	Hour	Summary of Events and Information	Remarks and references to Appendices
LESTREM	5th.		Transferred lines moved from BRAYELLE and Divisional Artillery with Coy HQ from LESTREM to R.11.a.4.8. shed 36A near PONT RIQUEUL. Construction of new bridge over LA LAWE river for full line hauled commenced. Patterning road diversions pencil craters and repairs to roads in forward areas. Weather hot. Enemy quiet.	A.B.9.
PONT RIQUEUL	6th.		Repairs to roads continued. Bridge over LA LAWE river completed. Heavy thunderstorm in afternoon. Enemy shelled area of hills about 5 p.m. No casualties	A.B.9.
Do.	7th.		Making road diversions round craters. Filling in craters. Night party worked on section of road Serains. Weather wet. No enemy action	A.B.9.
Do	8th.		Repair of roads continued. Erection of road Serains at night. Weather wet. Slight shelling of district at night. No Casualties	A.B.9.
Do.	9th.		Weather continued wet. Repair of forward roads. Erection of Brigade and Battn HQrs. Connecting Huts Shed at 59 Div School. Erection of road Serains at night. Latter were shelled during work. No casualties.	A.B.9.
Do.	10th.		Work on roads and road diversions continued. Carts making some trips and carriage tunnels for road serains. Serains erected at night, during enemy shelling. Construction of toda water packs at LUCHEUX continues. Weather wet. Enemy shelled neighbourhood at night. No Casualties.	A.B.9.

Instructions regarding War Diaries and Intelligence Summaries are contained in F. S. Regs., Part II. and the Staff Manual respectively. Title Pages will be prepared in manuscript.

Army Form C. 2118.

WAR DIARY Sheet 3

INTELLIGENCE SUMMARY

September 1918.

(Erase heading not required.)

Place	Date 1918 Sept M.	Hour	Summary of Events and Information	Remarks and references to Appendices
PONT RIQUEUL			Erection of Brigade H.Qrs. Soda Water Factory at LUCHEUX completed, repair of forward roads, and erection of road screens (night work). Weather wet. Enemy quiet. I.O.R. reinforcement arrived from R.E. Base Depôt.	A.B.7.
Do	12th.		Erection of Brigade H.Qrs. repairs to forward roads, erection of road screens at night has been continued. Night party were shelled and had 1 Casualty (O.R.) slightly wounded. Weather wet.	A.B.7.
Do.	13th.		Work as on 12th continued. Weather wet. Enemy quiet.	A.B.7.
Do	14th.		Weather again wet. Work on forward roads, and making road divisions, near Brigade H Qrs. Concealing plans Sk at 59 Druid School. Enemy quiet.	A.B.7.
Do	15th.		Weather improved. Work as on 14th continued. No enemy action.	A.B.7.
Do.	16th.		2 sections moved to forward hills at M.15.d.3.1. Shed 36A and employed clearing WINCHESTER ST. and NASSELDT ST. CT's. for passage of troops, and collecting duckboards, also preparation of bridges at R3, and R10 for demolition. Other work, improvements to forward roads and erection of Brigade and adviving HQs. Weather fine. Slight enemy shelling at night. No casualties	A.B.7.
Do	17th.		Repairs to and drainage of forward roads. Removal and disposal of enemy shell. Brigade HQ's continued. Clearing of O.P's. Weather fine. Enemy shells drained at night No Casualties	A.B.7.

WAR DIARY *of* **INTELLIGENCE SUMMARY**

Sheet 4

September 1918.

Army Form C. 2118.

Instructions regarding War Diaries and Intelligence Summaries are contained in F.S. Regs., Part II. and the Staff Manual respectively. Title Pages will be prepared in manuscript.

(Erase heading not required.)

Place	Date 1918	Hour	Summary of Events and Information	Remarks and references to Appendices
PONT RIQUEUL	18th		Work on Brigade HQrs; C.T's; and forward roads continued, also solving material for Battn. HQs. Camouflaging Plans Ste, 59 Divisional School. Weather fine. Enemy shells disturbed slightly. No casualties.	A.B.7.
Do.	19th		Improvements to Battn HQs, and Brigade HQs, C.T.s, and forward roads continued. Day fine with Enemy shelling at irregular intervals. No Casualties.	A.B.7.
Do.	20th		Work as on 19th continued. Enemy shelled forward billets, and obtained a direct hit on one shelter, killing 3 O.R. Day fine. Enemy shelled shelter of men billeted at night, but no further casualties.	A.B.7.
Do.	21st		Erection of trench foot centres, repairs and drainage of forward roads. Laying duckboards in C.T.s. Salving material for trench foot centres. Camouflaging Piano Ste @ 59 Divil School. Day fine. Slight enemy shelling, near billets. No Casualties. 3 O.R killed on 20th were buried at BOUT DEVILLE cemetery, R.24. a. 1.5., sheet 36A.	A.B.7.
Do	22nd		Erecting shelter for A.D.S. Work at 59 Divisional School completed. Laying duckboards and clearing C.T's. Marking trench foot centre. Weather dry. Enemy quiet.	A.B.7.
Do	23rd		Work on Battn. HQrs, Trench foot centre, A.D.S., Brigade Transport Lines, repairs to roads. Clearing and duckboarding C.T.s. Day fine. Enemy slightly shelled shelters. No Casualties.	A.B.7.
Do	24th		Work as on 23rd continued. Also new trench foot centre to outpost day and night. 1 Offr + completed. Enemy shelled shelters of men billets at night. No casualties. Day fine.	A.B.7.

WAR DIARY
INTELLIGENCE SUMMARY
Sheet 5 — September 1918

Army Form C. 2118.

(Erase heading not required.)

Place	Date Sept 1918	Hour	Summary of Events and Information	Remarks and references to Appendices
Pont Riqueul	25th		Work on A.D.S., Battalion H.Qrs, Brigade transport lines, repairs to forward roads, clearing of O.P.'s. Erection of board notices. Bombing School trade. Day fine. Enemy shelled Sheheid of Bullets at night. No casualties.	A.B.7.
Do	26th		Work as on 25th, also strengthening O.P. LAVENTIE, and erecting Battn Signal Office. Day fine. Enemy quiet.	A.B.7.
Do	27th		Continuation of work as on 26th. Weather fine. No casualties.	A.B.7.
Do	28th		Work of 26th continued, also making metal discs. Party commenced erection of Advanced Brigade H.Qrs at night. Weather fine. Slight Enemy shelling, no casualties.	A.B.7.
Do	29th		Making metal discs, and looked for Pack Saddlery. Strengthening O.P. LAVENTIE, erection of advanced Brigade H.Qrs, work on Brigade Stores continued. Forming three R.E. dumps in front line in preparation for attack, and reconnaissance of C.T.'s. to be dug to new front line after the objectives have been attained. Weather stormy. Enemy shelling at night, no casualties.	A.B.7.

In the Field

A.B. Few.
Major OC
467 Field Co. R.E.

30.9.1918.

Original.
467 Field Company
Royal Engineers
October 1918.

Army Form C. 2118.

WAR DIARY
or
INTELLIGENCE SUMMARY
(Erase heading not required.)

Vol 2.

Place	Date 1918	Hour	Summary of Events and Information	Remarks and references to Appendices
Pont Riqueul	Oct 1st		Company billets in farmhouse and cottages. Employed in clearing and opening new C.T. to front line. Heavy rain. Fair amount of enemy shelling and MG fire. No casualties.	O.P.
"	Oct 2		Company relieved from line work by 469 and 470th Field Coys. Day fine. No casualties	O.P.
"	Oct 2		Company employed on Brigade and Battalion transport limbs and preparing for move. Day fine. Enemy quiet.	No O.P.
"	Oct 3		Company move to Estaires, 4 Diamonds stationary. Day fine. No enemy action. 3 O.R. reinforcements.	O.P.
	Oct 4		Transport & Coy HQ moves from Estaires to Rouge de Bout. Company employed on dismantling huts and re-erecting same to Divisional HQrs Day fine. Slight enemy shelling. No casualties.	O.P.
Rouge du Bout	Oct 5		Erection of Divl HQrs continues, clearing roads & camp and camouflaging. Day fine. Enemy quiet.	O.P.

Army Form C. 2118.

WAR DIARY
or
INTELLIGENCE SUMMARY
(Erase heading not required.)

Army Troops Corp
Royal Engineers
October 1918

Sheet No 2.

Place	Date	Hour	Summary of Events and Information	Remarks and references to Appendices
ROUGE DE BOUT.	Oct 6		Work on Divl HQrs continued, also erecting HQrs for C.R.E. and new Divl Baths, Pack Store etc. Weather dull. Slight enemy S.P. Shell fire, no casualties.	
"	Oct 7		Work as on Oct 6th continued, also filling in craters in roads. Weather wet. Enemy quiet.	S.P.
"	Oct 8		Erection of Ordnance Stores, Brigade HQrs commenced, S.P. Divisional Baths, and HQrs continued. Weather wet. Enemy quiet.	
"	Oct 9		Work as on Oct 8th continued. Day fine. Enemy quiet.	S.P.
"	Oct 10		Work as on Oct 9th continued. Day fine. Enemy quiet.	S.P.
"	Oct 11		Work as on Oct 10th continued, also erecting new huts for A.S.M. Well at night. Enemy action nil.	S.P.

Army Form C. 2118.

WAR DIARY
or
INTELLIGENCE SUMMARY.
(Erase heading not required.)

467 Field Company.
Royal Engineers.
October 1915

Instructions regarding War Diaries and Intelligence Summaries are contained in F. S. Regs., Part II. and the Staff Manual respectively. Title Pages will be prepared in manuscript.

Place	Date	Hour	Summary of Events and Information	Remarks and references to Appendices
ROUGE DE BOUT.	Oct 12		Work on Dive Baths and HQrs continued. Erecting shelters to Infantry. Construction of stores for D.A.D.O.S. Wet at night. Enemy quiet.	W.
"	Oct 13		Work as on 12th continued, also erecting shelters to accommodate reserve Battalion. Rain. Enemy quiet.	W.
"	Oct 14		Work of 13th continued. Day fine. Enemy quiet. 1 Officer posted to Company.	W.
"	Oct 15		New advanced Divl HQrs commenced. Existing bridge over ditch strengthened to take lorry traffic and complete. Wet. Enemy action nil.	W.
"	Oct 16		Dismantling Divl HQrs and new advanced DHQrs continued. Approach and site cleared. Fine day. Enemy action nil.	W.

Army Form C. 2118.

WAR DIARY
or
INTELLIGENCE SUMMARY
(Erase heading not required.)

467 Field Coy.
Royal Engineers.
October 1918.

Commanding Officer: J.W.H. Mott

Place	Date 1918	Hour	Summary of Events and Information	Remarks and references to Appendices
ROUGE DE BOUT	Oct 17		Work on Div HQs continued dismantling huts and moving same to forward site. Company moved from ROUGE DE BOUT to Hutted Camp at FRY POST. Day dull.	W.
	Oct 18		Company moved from FRY POST to LAMBASSART. Day fine. Enemy action nil.	W.
	Oct 19		Company moved from LAMBASSART to FLERS. Day fine. Enemy action nil.	W.
	Oct 20		Company moved from FLERS to WILLEMS and employed repairing roads and road craters for 1st Line transport. Day fine. 4 Diamunkes Sections moved at night from WILLEMS to TEMPLEUVE.	W.
TEMPLEUVE	Oct 21		Removing mine charges from Church Tower TEMPLEUVE, filling in road craters, and repairs to roads for 1st Line transport. Forming Pontoon ferry over RIVER ESCAUT for passage of Infantry. Billets in village shelled by enemy. No casualties.	W.

Army Form C. 2118.

WAR DIARY
or
INTELLIGENCE SUMMARY
(Erase heading not required.)

Hqs Field Company
Royal Engineers
October 1918.

Place	Date 1918.	Hour	Summary of Events and Information	Remarks and references to Appendices
TEMPLEUVE	Oct 27		Transport and Coy Hqs left Williams in farm. Company employed filling in road craters, salving material, and arranging timber for rafts, making infantry footbridge over RIVER ESCAUT. Day fine. Enemy shelled town of Hellés heavily. Heavy M.G. and sniping fire encountered whilst working on footbridge, and 1 O.R. wounded, whilst on daylight reconnaissance. (W.)	
"	Oct 28		Unloading bridging materials and reconnaissance of site for same. Heavy M.G. and sniping fire during latter work. Day fine. No casualties. 2 rafts launched (W.)	
"	Oct 29		Filling in road craters, moving rafts to new positions, reconnaissance for new pack bridge, making trestles for new bridge. 2 half pontoons launches at night, both filled with cables and secured. Heavy M.G. and sniping fire which launching pontoons. No casualties. Day fine (W.)	

Army Form C. 2118.

WAR DIARY
INTELLIGENCE SUMMARY
(Erase heading not required.)

Hdqtr Field Company
Royal Engineers
October 1918.

Place	Date 1918	Hour	Summary of Events and Information	Remarks and references to Appendices
TEMPLEUVE	Oct 25.		Making trestles for new Oak bridge, framing rafts of German float, making gangways and ladders. Constructing new footbridge with 1 pontoon, and gangways to bank from pontoon on each side, completed. Construction of other new footbridge not possible owing to enemy action. Heavy I.M. shell fire W. 1 OR wounded. Day dull, night very dark.	
"	Oct 26.		Filling in road craters, cleaning ditches, framing up gangways, and making trestles for new bridges, repairs to footbridge. Reconnaissance of River sluices and wrote W. Level. Work on new footbridge commenced. Heavy enemy MG fire. Day fine. No casualties. Night intensely dark.	
"	Oct 27.		Loading and unloading parties for bringing materials, reconnaissance for new bridge and new tracks through wood. Repairs to new bridge, framing gangways and trestles for new bridge. Erection of cork footbridge completed. W. Heavy enemy MG and sniping fire during latter work. Night intensely dark. Heavy friend rain made work very difficult. No casualties.	

Army Form C. 2118.

WAR DIARY
or
INTELLIGENCE SUMMARY
(Erase heading not required.)

467 Field Company
Royal Engineers.
October.

Place	Date 1918	Hour	Summary of Events and Information	Remarks and references to Appendices
TEMPLEUVE	Oct 28		Filling in road craters and clearing ditches. Forming footpaths over RIEU DE LA TRUELLE, and RIEU DE WASMES. Making tracks thro' wood. Château grounds. Reconnaissance of RIVER ESCAUT and sluices. Framing trestles and gangways for new bridges. Examining sluices and opening same. Day fine. Heavy shelling particularly at night. No casualties.	
"	Oct 29		Reconnaissance to tracks for limbered traffic. Forming tracks throughout, footbridge for Infantry completed. (V) Repairs to raft, and bridge dismantled and renewed (V) in new site. Filling road craters & repairing roads. Day fine. Enemy shelling, no casualties. Night dark.	
"	Oct 30		Opening up tracks for limbered traffic, and making tracks thro' this wood for passage of Infantry. Filling road craters and clearing ditches, framing shoe transoms for new bridge. Night very dark. Heavy enemy shelling. 1 OR slightly wounded. Day fine.	

A. Miller Lieut for Major OC
467 FIELD CO R.E.

FIELD 31.X.1918

Original.

Army Form C. 2118.

WAR DIARY
or
INTELLIGENCE SUMMARY
(Erase heading not required.)

467 FIELD Cᵒʸ R.E. 1.F.

November 1918.

Sheet 1.

Place	Date 1918	Hour	Summary of Events and Information	Remarks and references to Appendices
TEMPLEUVE	Oct 31.		Company billeted in farmhouse and engaged in making tracks & G.S. limbers and erection of footbridges. Collection of timber for making rafts etc. Raftbridge erected with handrail and approaches made to same. (Infantry only). Day fine. Enemy M.G. and shell fire very heavy. Lieut Gibbs, 469ᵗʰ Cᵒ R.E. attached to this Coy wounded.	A.13.9.
Do.	Nov.1.		Work on G.S. limber tracks completed. Pathway made through woods. Reconnaissance of water lines etc. Evening gangways and making dummy gangway. Guide to transport. Day fine. Enemy shellfire again active. No casualties.	A.13.9.
Do	Nov 2.		Erecting posts and fences along path through woods. Erecting notice boards. Clearing road of felled trees and clearing cable ready for traffic. Repairs to roads. Firing in cradle. Day dull but fine. Enemy still very active. No casualties.	A.13.9.
Do.	Nov 3.		Company engaged in clearing road of felled trees. Repairs to roads and filling in craters. Preparing lashings etc. for new workings. Erecting new workings. Chess and trench boards completed, and approaches made. Day fine. Enemy M.G. and shell fire again very active, delaying work. No casualties.	A.13.9.

Army Form C. 2118.

WAR DIARY
or
INTELLIGENCE SUMMARY
(Erase heading not required.)

Sheet 2

Place	Date 1918	Hour	Summary of Events and Information	Remarks and references to Appendices
TEMPLEUVE	Nov 4.		Work today, clearing and repairing roads, clearing ditches. Oath through woods cleared and fires mended. Jamming paths on East side of river. Day fine. Enemy shell fire very heavy. No casualties	p. B.7.
Do.	Nov 5		Pushing new bridge for foot line transport over River ESCAULT and forming approaches to same. Parties attached to Infantry Bahls for special reconnaissance &c. Rain during day and am interval blocks night made work on bridge exceedingly difficult. Very heavy enemy M.G. and shell fire greatly hindered operations. No Casualties	A. B.7.
Do	Nov 6.		New bridge for foot line transport over River ESCAULT completed after about 30 hours continuous work. Other parties attached to Infantry Bahls for special reconnaissance. Day wet and night very black. Heavy enemy shell fire & gas am hindered work. No casualties	A. B.7.
Do.	Nov 7.		Company moved from TEMPLEUVE to SAILLY by route march, being relieved of the front line work by A69 Field Coy R.E. Parties worked on fitting up bustles for road bridge and handing over works to relieving Company. Day fine. Field duel. Enemy action Nil	A. B.7.

Army Form C. 2118.

WAR DIARY
INTELLIGENCE SUMMARY
(Erase heading not required.)

Sheet 3

Instructions regarding War Diaries and Intelligence Summaries are contained in F.S. Regs., Part II. and the Staff Manual respectively. Title Pages will be prepared in manuscript.

Place	Date 1918	Hour	Summary of Events and Information	Remarks and references to Appendices
SAILLY.	Nov 8.		Men. Company resting. Small party investigating FLERS church for suspected mine. Day fine. No enemy action.	A.B.F.
Do.	Nov 9.		Company had bathing parades. Onnees Coy clearing roads. Day fine. No enemy action.	A.B.F.
	Nov 10.		Full company moved by route march from SAILLY to RAMEGNIES CHIN. Day fine. No enemy action	A.B.F.
	Nov 11		Full Company moved by route march from RAMEGNIES CHIN to MOURCOURT, working on filling in craters and making road diversions round same for first line transport. Day showery. No enemy action. During the march news received the cessation of hostilities from 11 00 hours to-day	A.B.F.
MOURCOURT.	Nov 12		Company worked on clearing DIVNL roads, filling in shell hole etc. H road mines removed. Day fine.	A.B.F.
Do	Nov 13		Work as on 12th continued. Day fine.	A.B.F.

Army Form C. 2118.

WAR DIARY
INTELLIGENCE SUMMARY
(Erase heading not required.)

Sheet 4.

Place	Date 1918	Hour	Summary of Events and Information	Remarks and references to Appendices
MOURCOURT	Nov 14		Company worked on clearing DIVNL roads, filling in shell holes, cables &c. Day fine.	A.B.F.
	Nov 15.		Company moved with 176 Inf Brigade by route march from MOURCOURT to WILLEMS. Day fine.	A.B.F.
	Nov 16.		Company moved with 176 Inf Brigade by route march from WILLEMS to THUMESNIL. LEZ. LILLE. Day fine.	A.B.F.
THUMESNIL.	Nov 17		Company resting. Day fine	A.B.F.
Do.	Nov 18		do	A.B.F.
Do.	Nov 19		Company engaged clearing out Jackdaw in LILLE for a Divisional Club for NCO's and men. Day fine.	A.B.F.
Do	Nov 20		Training and fixing partitions, laying floors &c at Divnl Club. Day fine	A.B.F.
Do	Nov 21		do.	A.B.F.
Do	Nov 22		Laying floors, fixing doors and erection of bar at Divnl Club. do	A.B.F.

WAR DIARY
INTELLIGENCE SUMMARY

Sheet 5.

Army Form C. 2118.

Place	Date 1918	Hour	Summary of Events and Information	Remarks and references to Appendices
THUMESNIL	Nov 23		Worked Divisional Club. LILLE Continued. Laying wood floor, erecting stage in smokeroom, fixing stoves and making seats. Day dull.	A.B.7.
Do.	Nov 24		Divnl Club, work to day, fixing seats and stoves, laying wood floor in Cinema Etc. Day dull.	A.B.7.
Do.	Nov 25.		Work at club continued, and made ready for opening ceremony. Day dull. 2nd Coy on bathing parades.	A.B.7.
Do.	Nov 26		Work at Club continued. also cleaning Coy Quarters Etc. Day dull. 2nd Coy on bathing parades. N: 490511 Sgt Hall G.D awarded the Military Medal. D.R.O. 1841.	A.B.7.
Do.	Nov 27		ditto. Day dull.	A.B.7.
Do.	Nov 28		Worked Club continued, 1 section moved by motor lorry as advance party to BARLIN area. Rain all day.	A.B.7.
Do.	Nov 29		Work at Divnl Club continued. Day fine but dull.	A.B.7.

A. B. Few.
Major O.C.
467 Field Coy R.E. J J

Original

WAR DIARY
or
~~INTELLIGENCE SUMMARY~~
(Erase heading not required.)

467. FIELD. COY.
R.E.
December 1918.

Army Form C. 2118.

Sheet 1.

Instructions regarding War Diaries and Intelligence Summaries are contained in F. S. Regs., Part II. and the Staff Manual respectively. Title Pages will be prepared in manuscript.

Place	Date 1918	Hour	Summary of Events and Information	Remarks and references to Appendices
THUMESNIL	Nov 30		Men employed on Works at Union Jack Club. LILLE, and advance party repairing billets at BARLIN. Day fine but dull.	W.
Do	Dec 1.		Advance party to BARLIN. Day fine but dull.	W.
Do.	2nd		Work at Union Jack Club continued; advance party employed on repairs to Camp at BARLIN. Day fine.	W.
Do.	3rd.		ditto. Day dull. Lieut A.O.F. COBLEY awarded the MILITARY CROSS (authority 59. Div. R.O. 1865).	W.
Do.	4th		Work at Union Jack Club continued, and advance party to BARLIN engaged on repairs to Camp. Day fine.	W.
Do.	5th		Mounted section and Cyclists moved by March Route from THUMESNIL to FOURNES. Sappers engaged in clearing up billets, shelters Etc., prior to move. Day fine	W.
Do.	6th		Mounted section moved from FOURNES to BARLIN. Dismounted sections moved in motor lorries from THUMESNIL to BARLIN. Day fine.	W.

WAR DIARY
or
INTELLIGENCE SUMMARY

Army Form C. 2118.

Sheet 2.

(Erase heading not required.)

Place	Date Dec.	Hour	Summary of Events and Information	Remarks and references to Appendices
BARLIN	7th		Company killed in Miners hut Camp and worked on repairs and improvements to Camp in Brigade Area. Day fine.	W.
Do.	8th		Men engaged in carrying out repairs to R.E. Camp and transport lines. Day fine.	W.
Do.	9th		Repairs to Camps in Brigade Area and R.E. Camp. Day fine.	W.
Do.	10th		Men worked on making tables and forms for Educational Classes. Preparing huts for Cinema & Recreation Hut. General repairs in Brigade Area. Day med. 11 O.R. arrived from France 19 Sept.	W.
Do.	11th		ditto; also making huts for 2/1 Field Amb. Day dull and wet.	W.
Do.	12th		Dismantling huts and re-erecting same in R.E. Camp, filling up holes in Brigade area; repairs to A.I.B. Coy Stables. Day wet.	W.
Do.	13th		Work as on 12th continued. Day wet.	W.
Do.	14th		Repairs to Ranch Camp. Installers for Carpentry Classes. Fitting up huts for Cinema and repairs to Camps in Brigade area. Day Dull.	W.
Do.	15th		ditto, also repairs to R.E. and A.S.C. Stables. Day dull.	W.
Do.	16th		ditto, also Installers for Educational Classes in Carpentry and Injuineering. Day wet.	W.

WAR DIARY
or
INTELLIGENCE SUMMARY

Sheet 3.

(Erase heading not required.)

Army Form C. 2118

Instructions regarding War Diaries and Intelligence Summaries are contained in F.S. Regs., Part II. and the Staff Manual respectively. Title Pages will be prepared in manuscript.

Place	Date Dec.	Hour	Summary of Events and Information	Remarks and references to Appendices
BARLIN	17th		Work on Brigade Cinema; Pumping Stations; Repairs to Brigade Comps & Stables. Educational Class Instructors. Day fine.	W.
Do.	18th		Work as on 17th continued. Day wet.	W.
Do.	19th		Sinking huts for Cinema at HERSIN and R.E. Workshops. Instructors Eos for Education classes. Day fine.	W.
Do.	20th		General improvements to Camps on Brigade area and work of 19th continued. 3 O.R. Reinforcements from R.E. Base Depot. Day Dull.	W.
Do.	21st.		Fitting up Cinema Hut, HERSIN and preparing building for baths. Making table and forms for Brigade and Erecting Recreation Hut. Day fine.	W.
Do.	22nd		Work as on 21st continued. Day dull.	W.
Do.	23rd.		Making tables and forms, repairs to Cinema Hut, Instructors Educational Classes, fitting up Recreation Hut for R.E. Camp. Day dull and wet.	W.
Do.	24th		Work as on 23rd continued. 1 Officer from R.E. Base Depot arrives. Day dull and wet.	W.
Do.	25th		Christmas Day. No work. Day fine.	W.
Do.	26th		Boxing Day. No work. Day dull.	W.

WAR DIARY or INTELLIGENCE SUMMARY

Army Form C. 2118

Sheet 4.

Place	Date Dec.	Hour	Summary of Events and Information	Remarks and references to Appendices
BARLIN.	27th		Fitting up and repairing O.C.'s Camp. General repairs to Camps. Fitting up Cinelia hut at HERSIN. Day wet and stormy.	W.
Do.	28th		Work as on 27th continued. Instructors employed on Educational Classes and improving Cinema for R.F.A. HERSIN. Day wet.	W.
Do.	29th		Worked pumping stations, C.C.S. Camp and Instructors for Educational Classes. Reinorcements attended Church Parade Service. Day wet.	W.

Dec 29th 1918

C. Swan
Capt for Major O.C.
467 Field Co. R.E.

26 CERTIFIED COPY OF 467 FIELD Co. R.E.

WAR DIARY
or
INTELLIGENCE SUMMARY.

January 1919

Army Form C. 2118.

(Erase heading not required.)

Place	Hour, Date	Summary of Events and Information	Remarks and references to Appendices
1918	Dec. 30	Field Company moved by march Route from BARLIN to ST VENNANT being attached to 176 Inf. Bde. and under administrative instructions of 19th Corps. Day fine	Initials
	" 31	Company moved by march Route from ST VENNANT to HONDEGHEM and were billeted in Schoolrooms &c. Day fine with rain at night	A.S.
1919 HONDEGHEM	Jan. 1st	Sappers employed on work at 5th Army staging camp HONDEGHEM and carrying out general repairs to Company Billets and Stables. Day showery	A.S.
Do	" 2nd	Work of January 1st continued. Day dull and rainy	A.S.
Do	" 3rd	Work at 5th Army staging camp continued. Civilian repair of stables & billets fell through. Day dull & rainy	A.S.
Do	" 4th	Work of January 3rd continued. Also erecting cookhouse for R.B. & Q. Officers' mess. Day wet	A.S.
Do	" 5th	Sappers employed on erection of Cookhouse & messroom hut & stores annex at Army Staging camp HONDEGHEM. Remainder of Coy. Pickling. Day dull	A.S.
Do	" 6th	Sappers employed on Cookhouse &c completing footbridge over leat at EBFQ & Billets in Billets & billets in HONDEGHEM. Day fine	A.S.

Army Form C. 2118.

WAR DIARY
or
INTELLIGENCE SUMMARY.
(Erase heading not required.)

SHEET 2

Instructions regarding War Diaries and Intelligence Summaries are contained in F.S. Regs., Part II. and the Staff Manual respectively. Title pages will be prepared in manuscript.

Hour, Date, Place		Summary of Events and Information	Remarks and references to Appendices
1919			
HONDEGHEM	June 7	Lifting cement onto E Army Staging Camp – balloon Aviation sheds in E Army Staging Camp – shed for Repiling Point 176 Inf Bde – fitting up & repairing stalls & preparing Billets for No.7 Field Coy in HONDEGHEM – Day dull	D13.7
do.	" 8	Work of yesterday continued – site for re-erection of Y.M.C.A. hut preparing in E Army Staging Camp and 2 Armstrong huts re-erected in that camp – Day fine	D13.7
do	" 9	Work of 8th continued – material for Y.M.C.A. hut sorted out – Coy. Transport cleaned – Box Baths (run by 1 NCO and 1 man) open – shed for refilling point completed & Kaffee reinforcements from Base. Day fine	D13.7
do.	" 10	Work on E Army Staging Camp continued – day fine.	D13.7
do.	" 11	Work of 10th continued – Repairs to R.E. sheds – Coy transport picked & cleaned in readiness for move on 12th – Day fine	D13.7
do.	" 12	Company moved from HONDEGHEM by train to DUNKIRK – night of 12/13 spent in the train at DUNKIRK – day dull	D13.7
DUNKIRK.	" 13	Company entered MARDYCK Camp and was accommodated in tents – Company at disposal of D.O. MARDYCK for work and under administrative Orders of DUNKIRK Base I.C.R.E. DUNKIRK	D13.7
do.	" 14	Erecting Cookhouses & Latrines in Coy. Camp – drawing materials from D13.7 dump – day fine	D13.7

Army Form C. 2118.

WAR DIARY
or
INTELLIGENCE SUMMARY.
(Erase heading not required.)

Instructions regarding War Diaries and Intelligence Sheet. 3
Summaries are contained in F.S. Regs., Part II.
and the Staff Manual respectively. Title pages
will be prepared in manuscript.

Hour, Date, Place		Summary of Events and Information	Remarks and references to Appendices
	1919		Initialled by
DUNKIRK.	Jan. 15th	Sappers erecting hut for Officers mess & sleeping accommodation - setting out P. of W. Camp. MARDYCK and work on 14th continued - day dull & wet	DTBF
do.	16th	Work of 14th & 15th continued - erecting huts for 178 Infy Bde. and Ranger in demob. camp for clearing accommodation for demob. troops in MARDYCK Camp [day fine	DTBF
do.	17th	Erecting hut for Jinglo mess & quarters - hut for Officers mess & quarters - Ranger as Dining hall for demob. troops - laying water track to No 2 Camp party to HAZEBROUCH. RE. Dump for materials - setting out P of W. Camp & erecting mess Huts for Brigade - day fine	DTBF
do.	18th	Work on Officers and Jinglo Huts continued - work on Ranger Completed - erecting wire fence round P. of W. Camp and Huts for 178 Inf. Bde. Company bathed in morning - day fine	DTBF
do.	19th	11 Reinforcements from Base - first B. Category men to join the company - no work today - day fine.	DTBF
do.	20th	Sappers erecting huts for Company - Bde. HQ - Laying water main to No 4 Camp working on P. of W. Camp Day wild & wet	DTBF
do.	21st	Work as on 20th - day cold & fine	DTBF
do.	22nd	Work as on 20th (half day only) - day fine	DTBF
do.	23rd	Work as on 20th - day cold	DTBF

Army Form C. 2118.

SHEET 4

WAR DIARY
or
INTELLIGENCE SUMMARY.

(Erase heading not required.)

Instructions regarding War Diaries and Intelligence Summaries are contained in F.S. Regs., Part II. and the Staff Manual respectively. Title pages will be prepared in manuscript.

Hour, Date, Place	Summary of Events and Information	Remarks and references to Appendices
DUNKIRK Jany 24th 1919	Work as on 23rd - day fine	Initialled DSF
do " 25th	Half day - work as on previous days but in addition coal enclosure for 178 Brigade supply officer was set out - day fine	DSF
do " 26th	Day off for whole Company - day wet.	DSF
do " 27th	Work of Coy. same as previous days & party detached to dismantle hut at ZENENGHEM - site for No. 5 camp being prepared - day dull & cold.	DSF
do " 28th	Work as on 27th Day fine & cold.	DSF
do " 29th	Work on 28th continued - day dull & cold.	DSF
do " 30th	Work of 29th continued - day cold with snow.	DSF
do " 31st	Work as on 30th - day cold.	DSF
January 31st 1919	Signed DSF from Major OC 467 Field Coy R.E.	

Sheets 1-2-3-4 Certified true copy of War Diary for month of January 1919.

D. Arter - Capt
A/OC

467 (N.M.)
FIELD COMPANY,
R.E.
March 2nd 1919.

WAR DIARY
or
INTELLIGENCE SUMMARY

(Erase heading not required.)

467 Field Co. R.E. (T.F.)

SHEET 1   March 1919

Army Form C. 2118

Hour, Date, Place	Summary of Events and Information	Remarks and references to Appendices
MALDYCK CAMP, DUNKIRK. March 1st 1919	Company employed on erection of Huts No 5 Camp. Sinking wells - making Horse Drinking troughs. Erecting Huts for R.E. Day dull	
" 2nd	Sunday - no work - Day dull	
" 3rd	Work continued as on March 1st - Day rough.	
" 4th	Work continued as on March 1st - Day rough tuet.	
" 5th	Work continued as on March 1st also commenced new Ablution shed at Coy. Camp. Day wet and stormy.	
" 6th	no work this day on account of inclement weather	
" 7th	Company employed as on 5th. Day wet + dull	
" 8th	Work continued as on 7th. Day fine	
" 9th	Sunday no work. Day fine	

WAR DIARY
or
INTELLIGENCE SUMMARY

467 Field Co. R.E. (T.F.)

SHEET 2   March 1919

(Erase heading not required.)

Army Form C. 2118.

Hour, Date, Place	Summary of Events and Information	Remarks and references to Appendices
1919		
MARDYCK CAMP, DUNKIRK March 10th	Company employed in erection of Huts No 5 Camp - Sinking wells - erecting Nissen hut tabletin shed at Coy. Camp. - Day fine	AP
" 11th	Work continued as 10th. Day fine.	AP
" 12th	Work continued as 10th. Day fine.	AP
" 13th	Work continued as 10th. Day dull	AP
" 14th	Work as on 13th & in addition erecting Nissen Huts at R.E. Avenue, DUNKIRK DOCKS. Day fine.	AP
" 15th	Work as on 14th continued - Day showery.	AP
" 16th	Sunday - no work today. - Day wet & stormy	AP
" 17th	Work continued as on 15th - commenced painting huts in Coy. Camp. 2 Reinforcement O.R. arrived from CRE 59th Division. Day showery	AP
" 19th	Work continued as on 17th - commenced new Bath House at No. 2 Camp. Day dull	AP

WAR DIARY
or
INTELLIGENCE SUMMARY

Army Form C. 2118.

467 Field Co. R.E.

SHEET 3 March 1919

(Erase heading not required.)

Hour, Date, Place	Summary of Events and Information	Remarks and references to Appendices
1919		
MARDYCK CAMP DUNKIRK. March 19th	Work continued as 18th. and in addition forming a roadway across field to HOSPICE camp and erecting fence around Petrol Dump. also carrying out improvements to G.O.C's mess 178 Inf. Bde - Four Reinforcement officers arrived from 35th Division - Day fine	AP
" 20th	Work on 19th continued - commenced laying duckboard & painting huts in No.5 Camp. Fence around Petrol dump completed. Day fine	W
" 21st	Work on 20th continued - in addition erecting new Cookhouse in No.5 Camp. Day fine	W
" 22nd	Coy employed in: Breaker Mener Huts at R.E. Avenue DUNKIRK. Forming track across field to HOSPICE Camp. Laying duckboards between huts & erecting Cookhouse in No.5 Camp. Bath house No.2 Camp. Improvements to G.O.C's mess 178 Inf. Bde and commenced new brigade Horse Standings. Day dull & Stormy	W
" 23rd	Sunday - no work today - Day Stormy.	W
" 24th	Work continued as on 22nd. 24 O.R. Reinforcements reported from C.R.E. 59 Division. Day Stormy	W

WAR DIARY 467 Field Co. R.E. (T.F.)   Army Form C. 2118.
or
INTELLIGENCE SUMMARY.   March 1919
(Erase heading not required.)

SHEET 4.

Hour, Date, Place	Summary of Events and Information	Remarks and references to Appendices
MARDYCK CAMP DUNKIRK March 25th	Work as 24th continued - In addition 1 Sapper supervising erection of Ablution sheds stations by P.of.W. - Day dull - 2 Reinforcement P.O.W. arrived.	√
" 26th	Work on 25th continued except Mixer hut in R.E. Avenue - completed on 25th. Erection of tanks and carrying out water supply near HOSPICE Camp in addition - Day fine - 3 Reinforcements O.R. arrived.	√
" 27th	Work on 26th continued. Day wet & stormy. one reinforcement O.R. arrived	√
" 28th	Work on 27th continued - in addition framing more troughs for Brigade Horse standings & new Cookhouse for 176 Inf Bde - 3 reinforcement O.R. arrived Day fine but showery	√
" 29th	No work in morning owing to inclement weather afternoon Brickwork Twelves No 2 Camp. Framing Greenhouse & temporary work in P.O.W. Camp continues Day wet	√
" 30th	Sunday - no work today - Day dull	√
" 31st	Work of 29th continued - in addition - new Cookhouse for 176 & 178 Inf Bdes. Sheds to Latrines No 5 Camp - Wind very cold	√

April 1st 1919.

A. Swan - Capt. a/o O.C.

407 (N.M.) FIELD COMPANY, R.E.

WAR DIARY
INTELLIGENCE SUMMARY

467 FIELD Coy. R.E. (T.F.)

SHEET I

APRIL 1919.

Army Form C. 2118.

Hour, Date, Place	Summary of Events and Information	Remarks and references to Appendices

MARDYCK CAMP DUNKIRK 1919

April 1st — Company employed on Mardyck Camp - fitting up Bath House - No. 2 Camp - Laying duckboards between huts No. 5 Camp - Making brickwork troughs for Horse Standings. Erecting Cookhouses for 176, 178 Infantry Brigades. Improvements to GOC's Mess 178 Bde. Day fine.

" 2nd — Work as 1st continued - Linking well for hot & cold water Camp in addition. Day fine

" 3rd — Work of 2nd continued - except duckboarding No. 5 Camp. 4 reinforcements from CRE 59 Division. Day fine.

" 4th — Company employed on Cook Houses for 176, 178 Infantry Bdes. Water Supply for No. 3 & 4 Coy W Camp Bath House No. 3 Camp. Loading Bridging material in transport - Checking Bay Stores & Equipment. 58 OR Left Unit to report to CRE 1st Western Division & 1 OR to CRE 6th Division. All Volunteers & Retainables for Army of Occupation. Day fine.

" 5th — Work as 4th - erecting shed around Horsefall Distiller in 5 Camp in addition. Day fine.
Sunday - no work - Day fine.

" 6th —

" 7th — Work as on 5th continued - 2 Officers - Volunteers for A of O left Coy. - 1 to 141 A.T. Coy R.E. & 1 to Rotterdam R.E. District - Day fine.

WAR DIARY
or
INTELLIGENCE SUMMARY

467 Field Coy R.E.
April 1919

SHEET 2

Hour, Date, Place		Summary of Events and Information	Remarks and references to Appendices
MARDYCK CAMP DUNKIRK	1919		
	April 8th	Company employed on sinking well for 224 Coy R.A.S.C. erecting area for destructor No 5 Camp & Black House to 3 Camp. Water supply to 3H P. of W. Camp. Day fine.	do.
	" 9th	Work on 8th continued. Day fine.	do.
	" 10th	Work on 9th continued except work on No 5 Camp – with drainage No 2 Camp in addition – 1 officer left Coy – attached to Chief Engineer No 5 Area W.P. Day fine.	do.
	" 11th	Work on 10th continued – Day fine with high winds.	do.
	" 12th	No work today – owing to inclement weather.	do.
	" 13th	Sunday – no work – day dull.	do.
	" 14th	Company employed on Water supply to No 3 Camp Black House No 3 Camp – Drainage Nos 1 & 2 Camp fixing tank & at 224 Coy R.A.S.C. Camp. Day wet and stormy – 1 Reinforcement arrived from Base	O.I.
	" 15th	Work on 14th continued – day rough.	O.I.

WAR DIARY or INTELLIGENCE SUMMARY

SHEET 3   467 Field Coy R.E.

Army Form C. 2118.

Hour, Date, Place	Summary of Events and Information	Remarks and references to Appendices
MARDYCK CAMP DUNKIRK 1919 April 16th	Coy employed on Water Supply No.3 Camp - Drainage No.2 Camp - and loading up tools & equipment of units of the division - Day stormy	JLB
17th	Work of 16th continued - day fine	JLB
18th	Good Friday - no work - day fine	JLB
19th	Work of 17th continued. day dull	JLB
20th	Sunday - no work - day fine.	JLB
21st	Easter Monday - no work - day dull	JLB
22nd	Coy employed on Water Supply No.3 Camp. Drainage No.2 Camp - repairing & painting huts to R.E. Camp. 2 OR left Coy to report to CRE.12 Western Division - day fine	JLB
23rd	Work of 22nd continued - day fine	JLB

WAR DIARY or INTELLIGENCE SUMMARY

Army Form C. 2118.

467 Field Coy. R.E.

SHEET No. 4.

Place	Date	Hour	Summary of Events and Information	Remarks and references to Appendices
MARDYCK CAMP DUNKIRK	1919 April 24th		Work of 23rd continued — day fine.	J.S.
"	25th		Work of 24th continued — day stormy.	J.S.
"	26th		Work of 25th continued — day fine.	J.S.
"	27th		Sunday — no work — day cold with snow.	J.S.
"	28th		Work of 26th continued — day cold tokening.	J.S.
"	29th		Work of 28th continued — day even tokening.	J.S.
"	30th		Work of 29th continued — day stormy.	J.S.

J. Shaw
Lieut
for O.C.
467 F.C.

467 (N.M.)
FIELD COMPANY,
R.E.

Date April 30/19

Army Form C. 2118.

WAR DIARY
or
INTELLIGENCE SUMMARY

(Erase heading not required.)

467 Field Coy. R.E. (T)

Sheet No. 1

Place	Date 1919	Hour	Summary of Events and Information	Remarks and references to Appendices
MARDYCK CAMP. DUNKIRK.	May 1st		Company employed on works in MARDYCK CAMP. – Drainage works in No 2 Camp. Day stormy.	A
	2nd		Work of May 1st continued – day stormy.	A
	3rd		Work of May 2nd continued – day dull.	A
	4th		Sunday – no works – day fine.	A
	5th		Work of May 3rd continued day fine	A
	6th		Work of May 5th continued also erecting water storage tank and Military foreman of works day fine	A
	7th		Work of May 6th continued in morning – Inspection of water by Lt Col. Dumbeck in afternoon day fine	A
	8th		Work of 7th continued – Painting Company's transport in addition day fine	A
	9th		Work of 8th continued day fine	A
	10th		Work of 9th continued day fine	A
	11th		Sunday no works day fine	A

WAR DIARY
or
INTELLIGENCE SUMMARY
(Erase heading not required.)

467 Field Coy R.E.

Army Form C. 2118.

Sheet 2.

Place	Date 1919	Hour	Summary of Events and Information	Remarks and references to Appendices
MARDYCK CAMP, DUNKIRK	May 12th		Company employed on Drainage to D Camp, erecting watt storage tank until M. & S. – Painting company transport.. Dismantling Nissen hut in the 6 Camp for R.A.S.C. day fine.	
	" 13th		Work of 12th May continued day fine	
	" 14th		Work of 13th May continued – Re-erecting dismantled hut for R.A.S.C. day fine	
	" 15th		Work of 14th May continued day fine	
	" 16th		Work of 15th May continued day fine	
	" 17th		Work of 16th May continued – Re erection of hut for R.A.S.C. completed day fine	
	" 18th		No works today – Sunday – day fine	
	" 19th		Work of 17th May continued Water Storage tank completed day fine	
	" 20th		Work of 19th May continued – day fine	
	" 21st		Work of 20th May continued – day fine	
	" 22nd		Work of 21st May continued day fine	
	" 23rd		Work of 22nd May continued day fine	

Army Form C. 2118.

WAR DIARY
or
INTELLIGENCE SUMMARY
(Erase heading not required.)

SHEET No. 3   467 FIELD Co. R.E.

Place	Date 1919	Hour	Summary of Events and Information	Remarks and references to Appendices
MARDYCK CAMP DUNKIRK	May	24ᵗʰ	work of May 23ʳᵈ continued. day fine.	AD
	"	25ᵗʰ	Sunday no work. day dull.	AD
	"	26ᵗʰ	work of May 24ᵗʰ & 25ᵗʰ continued. Drainage work on no. 3 Camp in addition. day dull.	AD
	"	27ᵗʰ	work of 26ᵗʰ May continued. day fine.	AD
	"	28ᵗʰ	work of 27ᵗʰ May continued. day fine.	AD
	"	29ᵗʰ	work of 28ᵗʰ May continued. day fine.	AD
	"	30ᵗʰ	work of 29ᵗʰ May continued. day fine.	AD
	"	31ˢᵗ	work of 30ᵗʰ May continued. day fine.	AD

A. Oran.
Capt.
467 Co.

467 (N.M.)
FIELD COMPANY,
R.E.
No.
Date May 31/19

Army Form C. 2118

WAR DIARY
or
INTELLIGENCE SUMMARY
(Erase heading not required.)

No 64 Field Co. R.E.

SHEET No 1

Vol 29

Place	Date	Hour	Summary of Events and Information	Remarks and references to Appendices
MARDYCK CAMP DUNKIRK	1919 JUNE	1st	Sunday, no work, dry fine	7/8
	"	2nd	Company engaged on works in MARDYCK CAMP. Drainage work in No 3 Camp, dry fine.	13/8
	"	3rd	Work of June 2nd continued, dry fine	22/8
	"	4th	Work of June 3rd continued, dry fine.	16/8
	"	5th	Work of June 4th continued, dry fine.	4/8
	"	6th	Work of June 5th continued, dry fine.	14/8
	"	7th	Scene to U.K. proceeded to U.K., dry fine.	7/8
	"	8th	Sunday, no work, dry fine.	7/8
	"	9th	Guards & Camp duties (only 1 Offr & 13 O.R. remaining & Equipment Stores) dry fine	9/8
	"	10th	Duties of June 9th dry fine	4/8
	"	11th	Duties of June 10th dry fine.	7/8
	"	12th	Duties of June 11th dry fine.	22/8
	"	13th	Duties of June 12th dry fine.	2/8
	"	14th	Duties of June 13th dry fine.	11/8
	"	15th	Duties of June 14th dry fine.	7/8

Army Form C. 2118.

WAR DIARY
or
INTELLIGENCE SUMMARY
(Erase heading not required.)

SHEET No 2.   467 Field Co R.E.

Place	Date 1919	Hour	Summary of Events and Information	Remarks and references to Appendices
MARDYCK CAMP DUNKIRK	JUNE	16th	General & Camp duties. day fine	
	"	17th	Duties on June 16th. day fine	
	"	18th	Duties on June 17th. day fine	
	"	19th	Duties on June 18th. day fine	
	"	20th	Duties on June 19th. day cloudy	
	"	21st	Duties on June 20th. day wet	
	"	22nd	Sunday. Duties on June 21st. day cloudy	
	"	23rd	Duties on June 22nd. day fine	
	"	24th	Duties on June 23rd. day fine	
	"	25th	Duties on June 24th. day dull	
	"	26th	Duties on June 25th. day cloudy	
	"	27th	Duties on June 26th. day dull	
	"	28th	Duties on June 27th. day dull	
	"	29th	Duties on June 28th. day cloudy	
	"	30th	Duties on June 29th. day cloudy	

467 (H.M.) FIELD COMPANY, R.E.

Army Form C. 2118.

WAR DIARY
or
INTELLIGENCE SUMMARY
(Erase heading not required.)

SHEET No 1

JULY 1919.

464 Field Co R.E.

Vol 30

Place	Date	Hour	Summary of Events and Information	Remarks and references to Appendices
MARDYCK CAMP. DUNKIRK	July 1st		Company engaged on Sewers & Gang duties. Dry fine	
	2nd		Work of 1st continued. Dry fine	
	3rd		Work of the 1st continued. Dry fine	
	4th		Work of the 3rd continued. Dry duce	
	5th		Work of the 4th continued. Dry fine	
	6th		Work of the 5th continued. Dry fine	
	7th		Work of 6th continued. Dry duce. Received orders to move Transport to entrain at Gravelines on 8th instant. Dry duce	
	8th		Work of 1st continued. Packing wagons ready for Entrainment. Dry duce	
	9th		Work of 1st continued. Dry fine	
	10th		Wagons taken to Dunkirk docks ready for trucking. Dry fine	
	11th		Loading wagons on trucks, complete. Dry fine	
	12th		Sending wagons into Bergues, the evening. Rain in afternoon.	
	13th		Sunday.	

WAR DIARY or **INTELLIGENCE SUMMARY**
(Erase heading not required.)

Army Form C. 2118.

JULY 1919.

467 Field Co. R.E.

SHEET No 2.

Place	Date	Hour	Summary of Events and Information	Remarks and references to Appendices
MARDYCK CAMP	JULY 14th		General Holiday. 90 cowt. Day use.	
	15th		Engineers coming Transport into Range. Day shoeing. Closer Improved a/c. Day use.	
DUNKIRK	16th		Proceed to Convergation Reception Camp, Dunkirk. Day use.	